THE MORGAN HORSE

by Charlotte Wilcox

Illustrated with Photographs
by William Muñoz

C A P S T O N E   P R E S S
MANKATO

Capstone Books are published by Capstone Press
151 Good Counsel Drive, P.O. Box 669, Mankato, Minnesota 56002
http://www.capstone-press.com

Library of Congress Cataloging-in-Publication Data
Wilcox, Charlotte.
The Morgan Horse/by Charlotte Wilcox.
  p. cm.
  Includes bibliographical references (p. 46) and index.
  Summary: Discusses the unique horse, Justin Morgan, and the special breed
that carries his name and characteristics.
  ISBN 1-56065-362-0
  1. Morgan Horse—Juvenile literature. [1. Justin Morgan (Horse) 2. Morgan
horse. 3. Horses.] I. Title.
SF293.M8W55 1996
636.1'7—dc20   95-43910
                                                          CIP
                                                          AC

William Muñoz is a free-lance photographer. He has a B.A. from the
University of Montana. He has taken photographs of horses for this book
and many other books for children. William and his wife live on a farm
near St. Ignatius, Montana, where they raise cattle and horses.

2 3 4 5 6 05 04 03 02 01

Table of Contents

Words in **boldface** type in the text are defined in the Glossary in the back of this book.

Quick Facts about the Morgan Horse

Description

Height:
Morgans are 14 1/2 to 15 1/2 **hands** from the ground to the top of the shoulders. That is 58 to 62 inches (147 to 157 centimeters) tall. Horses are measured in hands. One hand equals four inches (10 centimeters).

Weight:
Morgans weigh 900 to 1,100 pounds (405 to 495 kilograms).

Physical features:
Morgans are small, muscular horses with short backs, arched necks, and long, thick manes and tails. Morgans are famous for their strength and endurance.

Colors:
They are **chestnut**, **bay**, brown, black, gray, **dun**, **buckskin**, **palomino**, and black dark chestnut (black with some red hairs). White markings are allowed only on the face and lower legs.

Development

Place of origin: Vermont and Massachusetts

Numbers: More than 130,000 Morgans are registered, with more than 3,000 added every year.

History of breed: All Morgan horses descend from one **stallion** who lived in Vermont about 200 years ago. The Morgan is the only breed in the world that is descended from just one horse.

Life History

Life span: A well-cared-for Morgan horse may live from 20 to 30 years.

Uses

Morgans can do almost anything. They are used for pleasure and trail riding, carriage driving, endurance riding, and farm and ranch work. They are the most popular breed of police horse. Morgans do well in all types of horse-show competition.

Chapter 1

A Very Special Horse

There has never been another horse like Justin Morgan. There probably never will be.

He could pull more weight than big workhorses. He never lost a race. He could beat the most famous racers of his day. His coat stayed soft and glossy all through the harsh New England winters. He worked hard. Sometimes he was abused. But he never turned mean.

The Sire of an Entire Breed

Justin Morgan was famous for many qualities. He had strength and speed. He had beauty and personality.

Morgan Horses have soft and glossy coats. This is a trait from the original Justin Morgan.

He became the **sire**, or father, of an entire breed of horses that still shows the characteristics of one original ancestor. No other horse has ever sired a whole breed.

Justin Morgan received some **traits** from his parents. But he was different from both of them. What was most unusual about Justin Morgan was his ability to pass on his best traits to his sons and daughters.

Most animals receive some traits from each parent. Justin Morgan's sons and daughters were mostly like him. They were very little like their mothers. Scientists call this special ability **prepotency**. It is very rare. Without this special ability, the Morgan horse breed would not exist.

Today there are thousands of Morgan horses all over the world. All of them descend from Justin Morgan. All show some of his traits and talents.

Morgans are some of the best all-around show and racing horses.

Chapter 2
The Horse That Could

The horse called Justin Morgan was born about 1790 on a farm in Massachusetts. No one knows the exact year. No one knows who his parents were, either.

One legend says that he descended from a beautiful bay stallion from Holland. Another legend says that his sire was a fancy **Thoroughbred** stolen from New York City.

When Justin Morgan was born, he was small. The farmer who owned him thought he would never amount to much. He was too small for the hard work expected of a horse.

In those days, horses pulled huge logs. They plowed rocky fields. They hauled heavy wagons. After working all day in the woods or fields, they carried their masters home on their

All Morgans have Justin Morgan's fine qualities of strength, beauty, and gentleness.

backs. On Sundays, they pulled a carriage to church. The farmer thought the little bay **colt** would never be able to keep up.

When the colt was about two or three years old, the farmer's cousin came to collect some money the farmer owed. The farmer gave his cousin a fine, big horse instead. The cousin was not sure he would get enough money for the horse to pay the debt. So the farmer gave him the little bay colt to make up the difference.

Justin Morgan and Figure

The cousin's name was Justin Morgan. He called the colt Figure. Years later, Figure would be renamed after the man who once owned him.

Morgan took Figure home to Randolph, Vermont. He rented him out to work skidding logs for a lumberjack. For skidding, the horse wears a work harness with heavy chains on each side. After the lumberjack cuts down a tree, he hooks the chains around the log. Then, the horse pulls the log out of the woods.

Justin Morgan is the only horse in history to father an entire breed.

The lumberjack thought Figure was not big enough for heavy work. He started him out skidding small logs. Figure surprised him. The little bay could do the work of a horse twice his size. Soon all the neighbors wanted to see what the pint-sized powerhouse could do.

Stronger than a Workhorse

One evening after a hard day of skidding logs, Figure was carrying his new master back to town. They met a crowd gathered near the sawmill. A gigantic pine log was lying near the road. Workers had been trying for hours to get it up to the sawmill. All the horses from town had given it a try. None could budge it.

The lumberjack knew he could profit from this situation. He took bets that Morgan's horse could skid the log all the way to the sawmill in three pulls. Figure's strength was well known around town. But no one believed the little horse could do it.

The lumberjack invited three men to stand on the log. This would make the log even

Some people wish that old Justin Morgan could have lived the happy life of today's Morgans.

heavier to pull. Everyone in town knew the little horse could never pull such a load.

The little horse bent his whole body forward into the pull. His muscles rippled with power. His hooves grabbed the dirt for traction. The log, with three men on top, started to move. Figure did not stop for breath until he had the log halfway to the sawmill. He skidded the log right up to the mill with just one more pull.

Racing Against the Thoroughbreds

Morgan's horse became a popular attraction at evening horse races. He could win any race. He could win by walking, **trotting**, or **galloping**. His fame spread.

Figure was challenged to race against two famous Thoroughbred racehorses from New York. The race was just a quarter mile (.4 kilometers). The real challenge was that Figure had to race the two Thoroughbreds separately. He had to win two races on the same day.

The American Morgan Horse Association keeps a register of Morgan horses born all over the world.

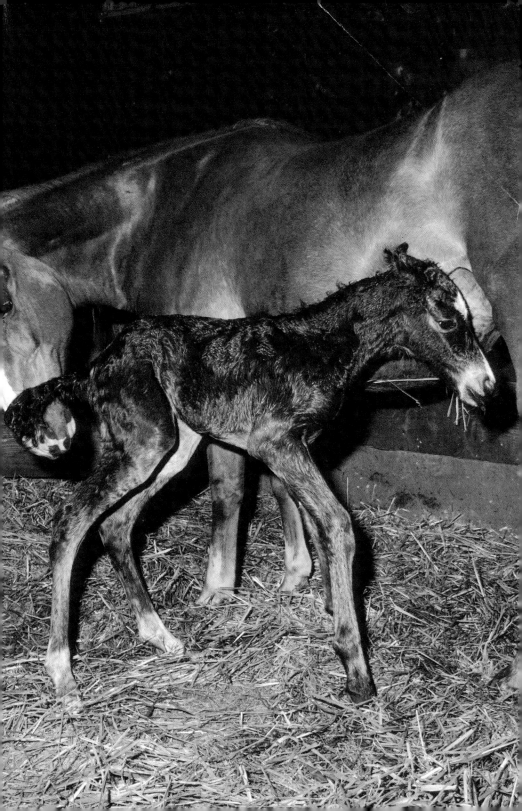

The New York horsemen thought they would have a sure win against the little Vermont logging horse. They were wrong. Figure beat both horses easily, one right after the other. When the races were over, Figure's owner challenged the New Yorkers to a walking or trotting race. But they did not want to race against Morgan's horse at any speed.

After a year of skidding logs and winning races, Figure went back to live with his owner, Justin Morgan. But his hard work was not done. Morgan was a traveling music teacher. For the next three winters, Figure carried Morgan from village to village to teach classes.

In the spring of 1798, Morgan died. He left his horse to the sheriff. The sheriff took good care of him but soon put him up for sale. The old lumberjack bought him. Figure was back to skidding logs all day and running races at night.

Morgans have short legs, but their bones are very strong. They are good for traveling over rough ground.

Famous as a Father

Figure was becoming a celebrity. People all over Vermont and Massachusetts wanted to bring their **mares** to him for breeding. They wanted to raise a **foal** like him. They were not disappointed. Figure became the sire of many fine horses. He made a lot of money for the lumberjack.

Unfortunately, the lumberjack could not handle money as well as he could handle a horse. He ended up in jail for not paying his bills. The lumberjack was forced to sell Figure to a farmer. Figure worked the fields, pulled the family carriage, and carried children on his back.

Figure had many owners after that. One put him in a six-horse team pulling freight wagons. Figure spent five hard years hauling heavy loads over mountain roads. Later he pulled a manure spreader on another farm.

When Figure was too old to work, he was sent to a pasture with other horses. He spent

Morgans eat 14 pounds (6 kilograms) of hay a day.

the last years of his life with no shelter and very little care. But not everyone forgot what a great horse he had been. People who saw him during the last year or two of his life said he still looked strong and proud. A lifetime of hard work and poor care never broke his spirit.

When Figure was about 30, which is very old for a horse, another horse kicked him in the side. No one saw or cared that his wound needed attention. Figure, probably the greatest horse ever born in North America, died unnoticed in that pasture during the cold winter of 1821.

Still, some would never forget Figure, later known as Justin Morgan. He had many sons and daughters throughout New England. They were loved and valued by their owners. Most of them had better lives than their remarkable sire. But they all looked just like him. They became a new breed that still carries the qualities of one of the greatest horses of all time.

Many Morgans are family riding horses.

Chapter 3

Growth of the Morgan

Justin Morgan's **offspring** attracted a lot of attention. Many of Justin Morgan's sons and daughters were used for breeding in New England. They all looked like him. They had his fine qualities of strength, beauty, and gentleness.

These horses passed on Justin Morgan's qualities to their own offspring and to their grandchildren. They all looked like old Morgan himself. No other horse in history had such an effect on so many generations.

The Birth of the Morgan Breed

Even while Justin Morgan was alive, the Morgan line was well known. At least six of Justin Morgan's sons were famous breeding stallions.

Morgans are famous for their strength and endurance.

Morgans are valued for their proud spirit.

Horse breeders crossbred Justin Morgan's grandchildren with some of their cousins. The colts had the good looks, abilities, and personality of the original Justin Morgan. It is not always wise to cross horses that are too closely related. So breeders kept careful lists of the family trees of their Morgan horses.

These family trees, called **pedigrees**, were kept at the farms where the horses were born. Sometimes breeders made copies for new owners when horses were sold. Through the years, some pedigrees were lost or forgotten.

In 1894, one Morgan breeder collected all the old Morgan pedigrees. He printed them in a book called *The American Morgan Horse Register*. This book encouraged many Morgan owners to search for their old pedigrees. A second Morgan pedigree book came out a few years later.

By this time, Morgans were popular throughout the United States. Many Morgans fought with the cavalry in the Civil War. Morgans made excellent police horses. They were beautiful carriage horses. They were comfortable riding horses. They worked hard. Morgans also herded cattle in the West.

Keeping the Morgan Alive

The automobile was invented about 1900. People no longer depended on horses. Hundreds of thousands of horses were killed or abandoned.

People wanted horses for only one thing. It was racing. Breeders began crossing Morgans with other horses. Horses that looked like old Justin Morgan were disappearing.

Morgans are known for their eager attitude.

In 1905, the U.S. government started buying **purebred** Morgans. The government wanted to keep the breed alive. Purebred means that the horse's pedigree is all from the same breed. It is not crossed with any other breeds. A government farm in Vermont soon began breeding purebred Morgans. The farm produced some of the greatest Morgans of all time. The farm is still in operation. It is now run by the University of Vermont.

Morgan Breeders Get Together

In 1909, some Morgan owners organized a club. It became the American Morgan Horse Association. The club held a Morgan horse show at the Vermont State Fair. Its goal was to promote the Morgan horse.

Today, the American Morgan Horse Association is a worldwide organization. It has thousands of members all over the United States and Canada. It also has members in Great Britain, Germany, Italy, Australia, and New Zealand.

The American Morgan Horse Association keeps a **register** of Morgan horses born all over the world. To be registered, a **veterinarian** must take a blood sample from the horse. A blood test proves who the horse's parents are. Both parents must be registered Morgans in order for the foal to be registered.

More than 130,000 Morgans are registered. Thousands of other Morgans have never been registered. But they all carry in their veins the blood of Justin Morgan.

Chapter 4

The Morgan Today

Purebred Morgan horses still look like Justin Morgan. They are a little bigger than Justin Morgan was. But they all still look like him.

What a Morgan Looks Like

Modern Morgans are not very tall. Horses are measured in hands. A hand is four inches (10 centimeters). A horse's height is measured from the **withers** to the ground. Most Morgans measure between 14 1/2 and 15 1/2 hands.

Morgans usually weigh 900 to 1,100 pounds (405 to 495 kilograms). Morgans have strong hooves. They are good for traveling over rough ground. Their legs are short but have very strong bones. They can stand up to a lot of hard

Morgans lift their feet high when they trot.

work. Because Morgans lift their feet high when they trot, people like them for horse shows.

Morgans have thick, arched necks. They have broad chests and strong shoulders. This is where much of the Morgan's strength comes from. Morgans have round bodies with short backs. Like the original Justin Morgan, they have thick manes. Their long tails often touch the ground.

Morgan Colors

Most Morgans are dark. Their colors are chestnut, bay, brown, black, and black dark chestnut. Light-colored Morgans may be gray, dun, buckskin, or palomino. Light colors are not as common as the dark colors. A horse of any other color cannot be registered as a Morgan. Morgans may have white markings on their lower legs and faces, but nowhere else.

More than 130,000 Morgans are registered with more than 3,000 added every year.

Loins

Flank

Hindquarters

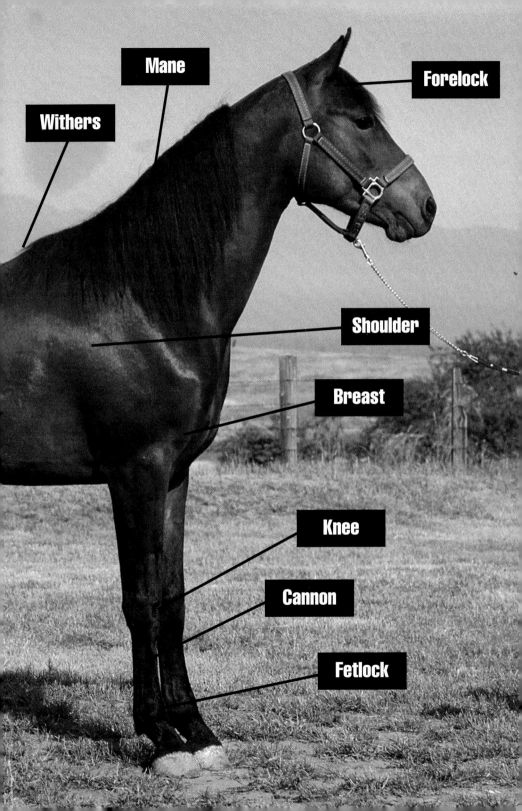

Mane

Forelock

Withers

Shoulder

Breast

Knee

Cannon

Fetlock

Chapter 5
The Morgan in Action

Modern Morgans do just about everything. Many are family riding horses. Some still pull carriages. Some skid logs and work in the fields like old Justin Morgan did.

Morgans in the Show Ring

One thing Justin Morgan never did was compete in a horse show. Morgan horses are popular with people who enter horses in shows. Morgans seem to do well in many different types of competition.

In one type of competition, horses are judged for their beauty. Morgans have glossy coats. Their manes and tails are thick and soft. Their well-formed bodies make them easy winners.

Morgans have well-formed bodies with thick manes and tails.

A Morgan's speed makes it a good competitor.

Morgans also do well in riding and carriage driving. People like their proud, high steps.

Morgans are especially good at jumping. There are jumps of different heights and shapes in a horse show. The jumps are set up in a ring. Judges rate how well the horse takes each jump.

Morgans in the Races

Morgan horses compete most often in two kinds of races. These are harness races and the **steeplechase.**

In a harness race, horses race around a track. They pull a small, two-wheeled cart called a sulky. A driver rides in the sulky. The horses trot as fast as they can. They must never break into a gallop. Trotting races are usually one-half mile (.8 kilometers) or 1 mile (1.6 kilometers). Each race takes only a few minutes. The Morgan's fast trot makes it a good harness racer.

The steeplechase is a difficult race. It is 2 to 5 miles (3 to 8 killometers) long. The horses must do more than run fast. They must also jump high fences and rows of bushes. They must cross streams and ponds. Morgans are good at the steeplechase. They are strong and jump well.

Morgans are also good at **endurance riding** or competitive trail riding. These are planned races that cover 25 to 100 miles (40 to 160 kilometers). The races can last for several days. They are often held in wilderness areas. The rough ground tests the horse's strength and ability. The horse also has to be fast to win the race.

Morgans at Work

Morgans make good police horses. They like to be around people. They stay calm in situations that might make other horses nervous. Morgan police horses are found in many cities.

Park rangers like to use Morgans for patrolling national and state parks. In Yellowstone National Park, Morgans take rangers into remote areas. The rangers check trails and boundaries and search for lost hikers.

Morgans are also popular carriage horses. Many places have horses and carriages with drivers for rent. People can go sightseeing in the city or take a quiet drive through a park. Couples getting married sometimes rent elegant carriages. The beautiful horses and dressed-up drivers take them to their weddings.

You can still see Morgans at work on farms and ranches all over North America. They plow and plant fields. They haul hay and herd cattle. Morgans are used to check fence lines and

Morgans may have white markings on their lower legs and faces, but nowhere else.

search for livestock. They pull wagons. They even skid logs.

Morgans on the Trail

Morgans are used more for pleasure riding and trail riding than for any other purpose. You see them in city parks and along country roads all over North America. They carry riders of all ages. After 200 years, the Morgan horse has found its place as the perfect all-around family horse.

Some people wish that old Justin Morgan could have lived the happy life of today's Morgans. They wish he could have taken children for rides or pulled a family carriage. But his life of hard work and dependable service helped make the Morgan horse what it is today. Families who own Morgans value them for their beauty, talent, and proud spirit. They also value them for their eager attitude in the face of challenges.

After 200 years, the Morgan horse had found its place as the perfect all-around family horse.

Glossary

bay—a reddish-brown horse with black legs, mane, and tail

buckskin—a tan horse with black legs, mane, and tail

chestnut—a reddish-brown horse

colt—a young male horse

dun—a tan horse

endurance riding—horse races that cover 25 to 100 miles (40 to 160 kilometers) and last for several days

foal—a young horse

gallop—the fastest movement of a horse

hand—a unit of measurement equal to four inches (10 centimeters)

harness—the set of straps, usually made of leather or nylon, that a horse wears to pull something

mare—a female horse

offspring—sons and daughters

palomino—a golden horse with a silvery-white mane and tail

pedigree—a list of a horse's ancestors

prepotency—the ability of an individual animal to pass on traits that override traits of the other parent

purebred—a horse that is fully one breed

register—to keep track of official pedigrees for a particular horse breed

sire—the father of a horse

stallion—a male horse

steeplechase—a cross-country horse race with such obstacles as fences, shrubs, and streams

Thoroughbred—a breed of racing horse that was bred in England

trait—a characteristic passed on from parents to children

trot—a medium-fast step natural to all horses, easily recognized by its up-and-down action

veterinarian—a person trained and qualified to treat diseases and injuries of animals

withers—the top of a horse's shoulders

To Learn More

Henderson, Carolyn. *Horse and Pony Breeds.* DK Riding Club. New York: DK Publishing, 1999.

Henry, Marguerite. *Album of Horses.* New York: Aladdin Books, 1993.

Kelley, Brent P. *Horse Breeds of the World.* Philadelphia: Chelsea House, 2001.

Pavia, Audrey. *Morgan Spirit.* Spirit of the Horse. Irvine, Calif.: Bowtie Press, 2001.

Spencer, Sally. *The Morgan Horse.* London: J. A. Allen & Co., 1999.

You can read articles about Morgan Horses in the following magazines: *Horse World, Practical Horseman, The Morgan Horse,* and *Young Rider.*

Useful Addresses

American Horse Council
1700 K Street NW, Suite 300
Washington, DC 20006-3805

American Morgan Horse Association
122 Bostwick Road
P.O. Box 960
Shelburne, VT 05482-0960

American Youth Horse Council
4193 Iron Works Pike
Lexington, KY 40511-2742

Canadian Morgan Horse Association
P.O. Box 286
Port Perry, ON L9L 1A3
Canada

Justin Morgan Memorial Museum
P.O. Box 519
3 Bostwick Road
Shelburn, VT 05482

Index